W9-BSW-168

Made by Me

Jane Bull

DK PUBLISHING

DK

LONDON, NEW YORK, MUNICH,
MELBOURNE, AND DELHI

For Stephen,
Charlotte, Billy,
and James

DESIGN • Jane Bull
EDITOR • Penelope Arlon
PHOTOGRAPHY • Andy Crawford

US EDITOR • Margaret Parrish
PUBLISHING MANAGER • Bridget Giles
PRODUCTION EDITOR • Sean Daly

First published in the United States in 2009
by DK Publishing
375 Hudson Street, New York, New York 10014

Copyright © 2009 Dorling Kindersley Limited
Copyright © 2009 Jane Bull

12 13 10 9 8 7 6
026-CD292 – 04/09

All rights reserved under International and Pan-American
Copyright Conventions. No part of this publication
may be reproduced, stored in a retrieval system,
or transmitted in any form or by any means,
electronic, mechanical, photocopying, recording,
or otherwise, without the prior written
permission of the copyright owner.
Published in Great Britain by
Dorling Kindersley Limited.

A catalog record for this book
is available from the Library of Congress

ISBN: 978-0-7566-5163-3

Color reproduction by Alta, UK
Printed and bound by L Rex Printing Co, China

Discover more at
www.dk.com

Made by Me

A book of lovely things to make...

Made by Me Workboxes

Pack away your odds and ends.

Before you go shopping for a workbox,
try looking around your home first.
Customizing a box that you find
is much more fun!

A lunch box
or mini suitcase
is ideal.

Handy tip

Decide what you want
to store in your box,
then choose one
that will fit your
equipment. Decorate
it with ribbons and
trimmings to make
it look like a
sewing box.

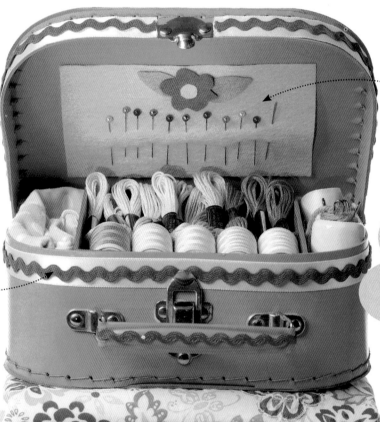

Glue a piece of
fabric to the lid of
the box to hold pins
and needles.

Glue on colorful
ribbons and
trimmings.

Use smaller boxes as
trays inside the case to
hold yarn and thread.

Workbox ideas

- **Snack containers**—tall tubes with pop-on lids are very good for storing your knitting needles.

- **Egg cartons**—they have a ready-made lid and are good for all the little things you need, like pins and needles.

- **Jelly jars**—collect jars and fill them with different things like buttons and threads. Decorate them using material and fabric glue.

A small container with a pop-on lid

Jelly jar

Turn the jar lid into a pin cushion.

Thread jar, button jar, pin jar—jars for everything!

You will need:

LOOK FOR this box on the pages in this book. It tells you what materials you need to make each project.

Egg cartons

Egg cartons are great because they have compartments inside them.

Attach felt flowers with fabric glue.

Snack boxes

These boxes are wrapped in fabric that's glued in place.

Embroidery

Learn the embroidery stitches and you can
decorate clothes, cushions—whatever you like!

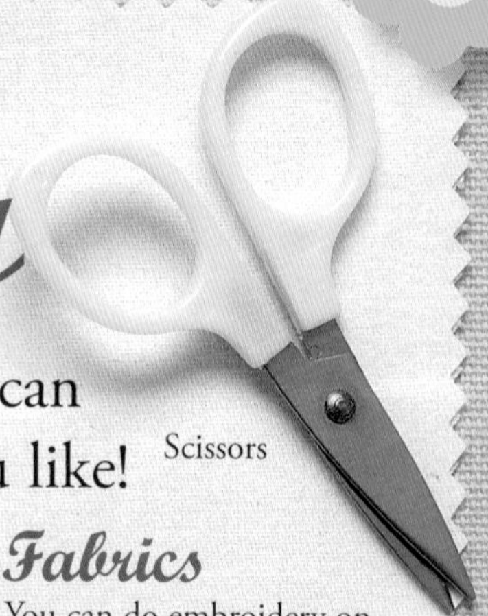

Scissors

Cotton
fabric

Tapestry
canvas

Aida fabric
for cross-
stitch

Rounded
needle

Pointed
needle

Fabrics

You can do embroidery on
all kinds of fabrics—from
jeans to T-shirts. The fabrics
shown here are cotton,
(which has a close weave),
tapestry canvas, and Aida,
(which has large holes and
is good for cross-stitch).

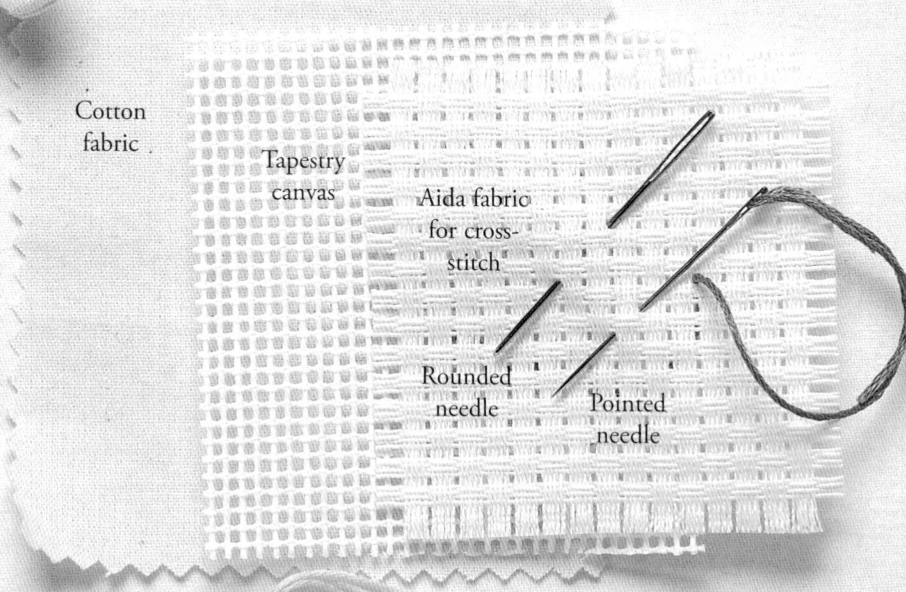

Needles

Embroidery needles have
large, long eyes with pointed
ends or rounded ends. Use
the pointed end when
working with close-weave
fabric like cotton and the
rounded end when doing
tapestry or cross-stitch.

Threads

Threads used in
embroidery are sold in
skeins. They are usually
made from cotton or wool.

Embroidery thread

This thread is made of
cotton and can be used
for most embroidery
stitches. Suitable for fine-
weave fabrics and Aida.

Tapestry yarn

This yarn is made of
wool and is used for
tapestry and coarse-
weave fabrics.

Embroidery thread

Tapestry yarn

A frame helps you to hold the fabric in place.

This fabric is calico. It's lightweight cotton and is cheap to buy.

Frames

Frames are used to stretch the fabric, so the area you are working on is flat and easy to handle.

Screw tightens large hoop.

Frames have two hoops—one inside the other. Separate the hoops and place the fabric over the smaller hoop. Then place the larger hoop over the top and tighten the screw.

Plastic hoop stretches over a smaller hoop.

Embroidery

What is it? Embroidery is stitching that enables you to create pictures and patterns. It can be used to decorate all kinds of fabrics using yarns and threads.

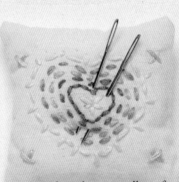

A pin cushion keeps needles safe.

Practice your design on paper first.

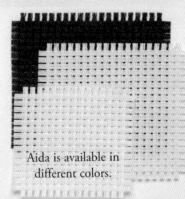

Aïda is available in different colors.

Picture stitches

Transfer your doodles onto fabric.
Then embroider over the lines to make
pretty stitched pictures.

You will need:
- embroidery frame
- skeins of embroidery silk
- embroidery needle
- fabric

Work out your
design on
paper first.

Put the fabric
in the frame.

Copy your design
onto the fabric.

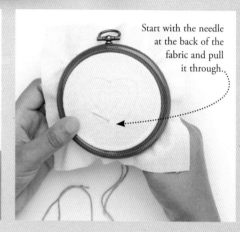

Start with the needle
at the back of the
fabric and pull
it through.

Pull the thread
through to
the knot.

Knot the end
of the thread.

Stitch along
the pencil lines,
(see page 16 to
see how to do
running stitch).

To finish off a color, turn
the frame over...

... slip the
thread back
through the last
stitches and cut
off the end.

Begin and end colors
in the same way.

Remove the
frame when
you have
finished.

Now the fabric is ready
to use for a project.

Backstitch

Lazy daisy stitch

Running stitch

Stitch directory

Go to page 16 to learn how to do these fancy stitches.

Chain stitch

Cross-stitch

Cross-stitch

Running stitch

Blanket stitch

T-shirt

It's time to dress up your clothes!

Turn a white T-shirt into a work of art with buttons, bows, and stylish stitching. You can even pin on other projects in this book as beautiful brooches.

Patterns

Use the patterns at the front of the book to make your own pretty decorations.

Buttons

Whenever you see a stray button, put it into your sewing kit. Buttons add sparkle to all kinds of designs—and if you find them, they're free!

Cross-stitch

Blanket
stitch

Cupcakes
(see page 36)

Chain
stitch

Running
stitch

Blanket
stitch

Pocket locket
(see page 28)

Handy tip
Work out your designs
on paper before you sew
them onto your T-shirt.
(See pages 16 and 17
for stitch decorations.)

Running
stitch

Stitch directory

These are the stitches that you use throughout the book.

Stitching tip
Try and keep your stitches even and neat.

Running stitch

This creates a dotted line—simply push the needle in and out of the fabric. Start by making a knot in the end of the thread.

2. Push the needle down and up through the fabric and pull to make a stitch.

START HERE
1. Pull the needle up through the fabric to the knot.

Backstitch

This makes a continuous line of stitches—unlike a running stitch, you go back to fill the gap between the stitch each time.

2. Start as if you are doing a running stitch, then take the needle back to the end of the last stitch.

3. Bring the needle back up here.

START HERE
1. Pull the needle up through the fabric to the knot.

Lazy daisy stitch

This pretty stitch is very useful for embroidery decoration. Draw out your daisy design first in light pencil, then follow the lines with your stitches.

2. Now bring it up through another petal until you have finished the flower.

1. Tie a knot in your thread and pull it up through the beginning of a petal and down at the end.

Chain stitch

This is a very useful decorating stitch—great for flower stems and leaves. You may need to practice the stitch to get it just right.

1. Tie a knot in the thread and pull it up through the fabric.

2. Now push the needle back down next to the thread.

3. Don't pull it tight; leave a little loop.

4. Now bring the needle up through the loop and pull the thread through.

5. Repeat stages 1 to 4. Keep the stitches as even as possible.

Practice a chain stitch on a curved line so you can make shapes.

Blanket stitch

This stitch is good for making neat, decorative edges and for sewing one piece of fabric to another.

1. Tie a knot in the thread and pull the needle up through the fabric.

2. Push the needle back through next to the stitch and up below it, making sure the loose end is caught, as shown.

3. Push the needle down and up again so it is the same size as the previous stitch, catching the loose thread again.

4. Repeat these steps to make more loops.

Cross-stitch

You can make whole pictures using a cross-stitch (see page 20).

Draw out crosses in light pencil on your fabric.

Sew a line of crosses from left to right in one direction...

... then finish them off by sewing back the other way.

Decorate a T-shirt

You need to use an embroidery needle with a big eye.

Use the stitches on this page to jazz up your T-shirt. And try decorating bags, jeans pockets, and any other clothes, too.

Embroidery thread

Flatten the end of the thread to help it go through the eye of the needle.

Knot the end.

Finish stitching

On the back of the fabric, push the needle through the loop of the last stitch.

Pull the thread tight and repeat to make it secure.

Blanket-stitch edging

Blanket stitch the edge of the T-shirt using the seam as a guide.

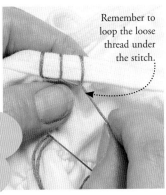

Remember to loop the loose thread under the stitch.

Draw on designs

Practice drawing your designs onto paper first. Then copy the pattern onto your T-shirt in pencil—this will disappear when you wash your shirt.

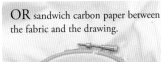
Use a pencil to draw your design onto the fabric...

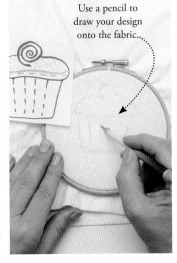

OR sandwich carbon paper between the fabric and the drawing.

Trace over your design to transfer it onto the fabric.

Stitch your design following the marks on the fabric...

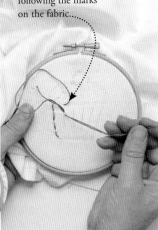

Sew on a button

Push the needle up through the spot where you want the button to be.

Then thread the button onto the needle and drop it down the thread.

Sew down through the other button hole and the fabric, then up again through the first hole.

Repeat this five more times.

Finish off at the back of the fabric and wind the thread around the back of the button twice.

Then pass the needle through the middle of the stitches.

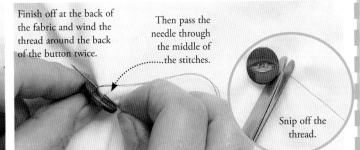
Snip off the thread.

Pixel pix

Tapestries are made up of
little squares, just like pixels on a computer. Try making pictures where each stitch is like a pixel.

Tapestry yarn

Handy tip
Always use thick tapestry yarn—it won't leave gaps between the stitches.

Sew a picture

Draw a picture on graph paper, making sure you use the squares as the outline of the shape.

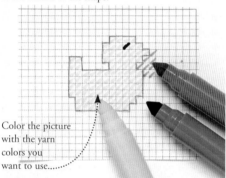

Color the picture with the yarn colors you want to use.....

Carefully transfer the colors onto some tapestry canvas.

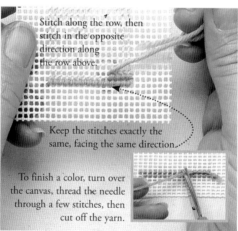

......Each stitch will be stitched at an angle.

Embroidery needle with a rounded end

Tapestry canvas

Cut a length of yarn, thread the needle, and knot the end.

.....Pull the needle up through the canvas then down through the diagonal stitch above to the right.

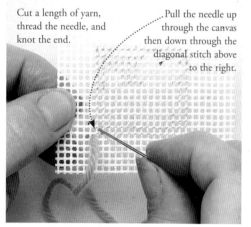

Stitch along the row, then stitch in the opposite direction along the row above.

Keep the stitches exactly the same, facing the same direction.

To finish a color, turn over the canvas, thread the needle through a few stitches, then cut off the yarn.

Graph paper

Begin the next color, working along the rows as before.

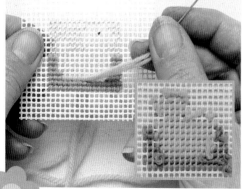

Keep changing colors until you have finished your picture.

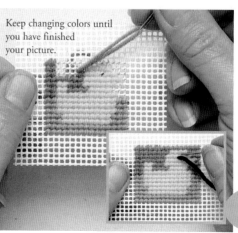

Scissors

If you don't have graph paper, draw squares yourself using a ruler.

It's a gift
Make a pixel picture for a special present. You could frame one, or turn one into a brooch or key ring.

To practice, try stitching patterns rather than pictures.

Cross-stitch

Crisscross, crisscross.

Cross-stitch is so easy and as long as you keep the designs simple, it will look good enough to hang on a wall! You can even write in cross-stitch.

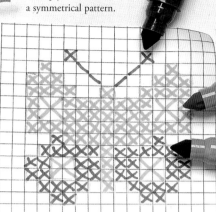

Use graph paper to help you draw a symmetrical pattern.

Color in your picture.

1 Draw a picture

Aida fabric

Embroidery frame

Embroidery needle with a rounded end

Embroidery thread

2 Collect your materials

Put the fabric into the frame.

Use a pencil to draw your design onto the fabric.

3 Transfer your design

See page 16 for cross-stitch instructions.

Stitch over your design.

Stitch in rows as much as possible.

4 Start stitching

Remove the frame and straighten out the fabric...

... or use the embroidery frame as a picture frame.

Gather up the fabric at the back and sew in place.

5 Finish it off

Sampler

A sampler is a piece of fabric that you practice on. Experiment with different sized cross-stitches and different colored threads. With this type of fabric you don't always need a picture frame.

When you have finished, fray the edge of the fabric to make it look pretty.

Little mats

Samplers make lovely little mats, too. When you've finished stitching, glue them onto felt.

Pins

Sewing

Here you'll find out how to make bags and pouches, and how to make fabulous fabric jewelry, too!

Safety pins

Buttons for decorating and fastening

Pins

Pins help hold fabrics together and safety pins are useful for threading ribbons.

Felt

Corduroy

Cotton

Use pinking shears to stop the edges of the fabric from fraying.

Fabric

The projects in this book mainly use lightweight cotton and felt. Felt is good since it doesn't fray at the edges. There are other fabrics to choose from, too, including corduroy.

Needles

Sewing needles are small and thin with a round eye. Choose a medium-sized needle for your work.

Scissors

Use a tape measure to check your fabric is the right size.

Tape measure

Needle threader

Sewing thread

This is made of cotton and can be used for all the sewing projects here. Use a needle threader if you have trouble pushing the thread through the eye.

Thread

Trimmings

Trimmings, such as ribbons and lace edging, finish off your projects perfectly.

Ribbons and lace

Pin cushion

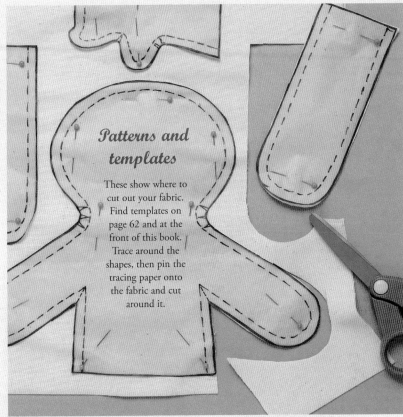

Patterns and templates

These show where to cut out your fabric. Find templates on page 62 and at the front of this book. Trace around the shapes, then pin the tracing paper onto the fabric and cut around it.

Sewing

What is sewing? Sewing is stitching to decorate or connect together pieces of fabric. When you sew you can make toys, bags, and clothes.

Fun with felt

Felt is great to use as decoration and comes in all kinds of different colors.

Sewing

Pinking shears

These scissors don't just give a decorative edge to your fabric...

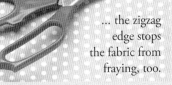

... the zigzag edge stops the fabric from fraying, too.

Pouches

Bags for everything—from little ones to hold your hair clips to big ones for your shoes.

Fold the fabric over by $1/2$ in (13 mm).

Sew the fold down using a running stitch.

1 Cut out the fabric

As a guide, cut out a piece of fabric 4 in x 7 in (10 cm x 17 cm).

Fold edge.

Fold the fabric in half, right sides together, and pin in place.

Sew up the two edges using running stitch. Leave the top open.

You will need:
- cotton fabric (see steps for size)
- sewing thread
- needles and pins
- safety pin
- ribbon

2 Stitch it up

Turn the bag right side out.

3 Turn right side out

Push the safety pin through the gap in the end.

Cut a piece of ribbon 12 in (30 cm) long.

Attach a safety pin to the end of the ribbon.

Handy pins

Attaching a safety pin to the end of the ribbon gives you something solid to guide through the fabric.

Work the pin around until it comes through the other side, then remove the pin.

4 Cut the ribbon

5 Thread the ribbon

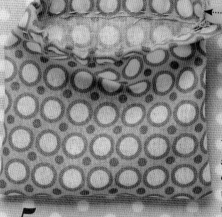

Ribbon ties

When you have threaded the ribbon, tie the two ends together so they can't slip out. Push the material along the ribbon to close the bag.

Big bag

Cut a piece of fabric 20 in x 10 in (50 cm x 25 cm).

Medium bag

Cut a piece of fabric 16 in x 8 in (40 cm x 20 cm).

You could try

Stitch your friend's name on a bag and fill it with wrapped candies. It'll make a perfect present!

Baby bag

Cut a piece of fabric 4 in x 7 in (10 cm x 17 cm).

Lavender bags

Dried lavender flowers....

Dried lavender...

Lavender smells beautiful. The dried flowers give off a strong scent—they're perfect for stuffing these little pyramid bags.

Put the right sides together.

1 Cut out fabric

Cut two squares of thin fabric 4 in x 4 in (10 cm x 10 cm).

Sew around three edges using backstitch (see page 16).

You will need:
- cotton fabric
- needle, pins, and thread
- dried lavender flowers
- dried rice

Fill the bag with two tablespoons of dried rice and one tablespoon of dried lavender flowers.

Turn the bag right side out....

Don't stuff it too full.

2 Turn the right side out

3 Fill up the bag

If you cut your fabric squares smaller, you can make mini pyramids, too.

To finish, bring the sides of the bag together to make a triangle shape.

Turn in the edges and neatly stitch them together.

Sew on pretty ribbon or trimming and stitch into place.

Handy tip Use fabric glue to hold the decorations in place.

4 Stitch together

5 Finishing touch

Sweet smells

If you can't find dried lavender, potpourri makes a good alternative—scents like roses or pine work well.

You could try

Personalize your bag by using the embroidery stitches you've learned from the embroidery section. Sew your design to the front before you sew the squares together at step 1.

Pocket lockets

More than just pretty pendants!

They are the perfect place to keep your keys. Just slide the felt sleeve up and down the ribbon to use or hide your key.

Try it out

You will need:
- felt shapes cut to size (use the patterns at the front of the book)
- skein of embroidery silk
- embroidery needle
- pins
- ribbon—long or short

Tie the ribbon into a big knot that won't slip through the felt sleeve........

Position the ribbon between the felt pieces.

Pin the felt and ribbon together....

Use blanket stitch (see page 16) to sew the back and front together. Make sure you don't sew through the ribbon.

Pull the sleeve up and down the ribbon to hide or show the key........

Cut two felt shapes for the key sleeve.

Cut some felt shapes for decoration.

Sew the shapes to the front felt piece.

Loop the ribbon through the key.

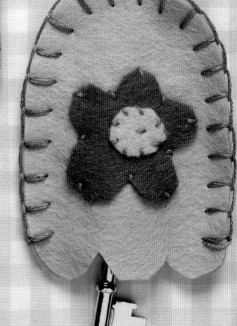

1 *Sew on decoration*

2 *Sew up the sides*

3 *All done!*

Dotty

Fancy stitches
Experiment with the
embroidery stitches that
you'll find earlier in
the book.

Daisy

Owl

Key pendants
Make sure the ribbon is
long enough to fit
around your neck, or
short enough to wear
on your wrist.

Chimp

Hanging softies

Make a collection of mini padded shapes
and hang them absolutely everywhere!

You will need:
- felt shapes cut to size (use the patterns at the front of the book)
- skeins of embroidery silk
- embroidery needle
- stuffing

Back shape

Front shape

Cut out some hearts

Decoration

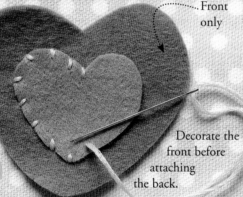

Front only

Sewing tip
Keep your stitches the same size and evenly spaced apart.

Decorate the front before attaching the back.

1 Sew on the decorations

Front and back

Join the front and the back together using a blanket stitch (see page 16), leaving a small gap.

2 Sew the hearts together

Fill the shape with stuffing— but not too full.

3 Stuff it

Sew up the gap and fasten off.

4 Stitch together

Templates
Use the patterns at the front of the book—or make up your own.

Hang up

Add embroidery silk
or a ribbon and you can
hang a softie anywhere—
on the Christmas tree,
a door knob...

Gift ideas

• **Brooch**—Sew a safety
pin to the back of a softie.
• **Key ring**—Attach your
softie to your key ring.
• **Necklace**—Use ribbon
to turn a softie into
something to wear.

Felt flowers

Pretty petals
are a perfect finish for a party
outfit. Pin them to hair clips,
hair bands, bangles,
and bags.

You will need:
- felt shapes cut to size (use the patterns at the front of the book)
- needle and sewing thread
- buttons

Make a flower

1. Make a petal-shaped template, then make five felt petals.

Draw around cardboard.

2. Cut out the petals.

3. Sew the petals together using a running stitch (page 16).

4. Sew the last petal to the edge of the first one.

5. Pull the thread carefully to gather up the fabric petals.

6. Sew through the gathers to hold them together.

Hair clips

Hair ties

Finishing touches

1. Make another flower. Stitch through the flowers' centers.

2. Attach them by sewing on a button (see page 17).

3. Sew or glue onto a hair band, hair clip, or a bangle.

Handy tip

These flowers are a really handy way of using up your scraps. When you make a felt project, keep the little pieces to make lots of colored flowers.

Fashion flowers

Use these fancy flowers to decorate your clothes and bags.

Bags of Ribbons

All the trimmings—collect up lots and lots of ribbon scraps and turn them into multicolored bags.

You will need:
- two squares of material—lightweight cotton for the front and heavier cotton for the back
- sewing thread
- needle and pins
- lots of ribbon scraps

BAG BACK Use a thick fabric 4 in x 4 in (10 cm x 10 cm)

BAG FRONT Use light cotton 4 in x 4 in (10 cm x 10 cm).

Cut lots of pieces of ribbon the same width as the fabric.

1 Collect up the pieces

Ribbons
Look for ribbons on presents and packaging and start collecting them. Even small lengths can be used to decorate your projects.

Sew the first ribbon at the bottom.

Fold over the top to make it neat and hem in place using little stitches.

2 Sew on the ribbon

Sew the last piece of ribbon over the folded edge.

Add lace and other trimming as well.

3 Add some trimmings

Place the right sides together.

Sew round three sides using backstitch (see page 16).

Fold over the top to make it neat, then hem it.

4 Join the front and back

5 Turn right side out

Add a strap

Cut a piece of ribbon long enough to hang the bag from your shoulder. Sew it to the sides of the finished bag.

Ribbon strap

Big or small

The size of this bag is just a guide. You can make the bag as big or as little as you like. Decide what you want to carry around and make a bag to fit it.

You could use buttons to attach the strap.

Cupcakes

They look good enough to eat! These little cupcakes can be delicious pin cushions, tasty brooches, or simply look scrumptious on a plate.

You will need:
- felt shapes cut to size (use the patterns at the front of the book)
- skeins of embroidery silk
- embroidery needle
- stuffing

Back shape

Front shape

Decoration

1 *Cut out some pastry*

Front only

Use lots of little short stitches.

2 *Sew on the jam*

Place the front and back together.

Sew the front and back together.

3 *Stitch together*

Leaving a small gap, pull the thread to gather up the fabric.

4 *Gather it up*

Fill it with stuffing—but not too much.

Open up the pie for the filling.

5 *Stuff the jam tart*

Sew up the gap and fasten off.

6 *Stitch it up*

Cherry pie
Cut a red felt circle for the cherry.

Jam tart
Yellow stitches look like little seeds.

Chocolate cake
Cut a swirl of pink felt for icing.

Sprinkle-topped cake
Colorful stitches look like sprinkles.

Brooches
Sew a safety pin to the back.

Pin cushion

Gift ideas
• **Brooch**—Sew a safety pin to a mini cupcake.
• **Pin cushion**—Put in your sewing kit as a pin cushion.
• **Birthday cake**—Give one to a friend to celebrate a special occasion!

Hello Dolly!

Dolly's awake!
Pack up her nightgown, put on her clothes, and she's ready for the day ahead.

Dolly's bag

Make a pretty pouch to keep Dolly in—find out how on page 24.

Dolly's dressed up for the day.

These are Dolly's night-time things.

Goodnight Dolly!

Shhh, Dolly's asleep.

Take out her pillow, put on her nightgown, and Dolly
is ready for bed. And don't forget her teddy bear!

Dolly's
pillow

Dolly's
nightgown

Dolly's
teddy
bear

Two dolls
in one

These two dolls are really
one doll! One side of her
head has an awake face.
Turn her over for her
sleeping face.

Make your own two-sided doll

Snip and sew your own "Hello/Goodnight Dolly." Use plain cotton fabric and the pattern on page 62.

You will need:

- Dolly pattern
- cotton fabric
- pins
- scissors
- sewing thread
- stuffing
- embroidery thread
- pencil

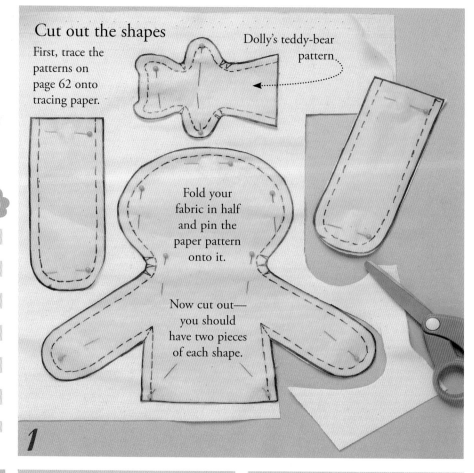

Cut out the shapes

First, trace the patterns on page 62 onto tracing paper.

Dolly's teddy-bear pattern

Fold your fabric in half and pin the paper pattern onto it.

Now cut out— you should have two pieces of each shape.

1

Remove the paper and pin the two pieces of fabric together.

Stitch the shapes together.

2

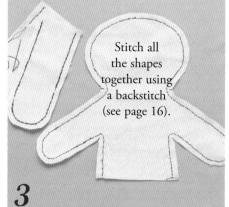

Stitch all the shapes together using a backstitch (see page 16).

3

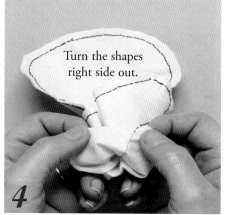

Turn the shapes right side out.

4

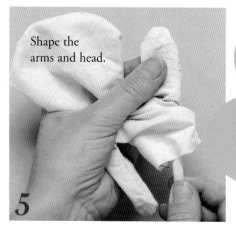

Shape the arms and head.

5

Handy tip

Use a blunt pencil to help shape your doll. Push gently and carefully so you don't break the stitching.

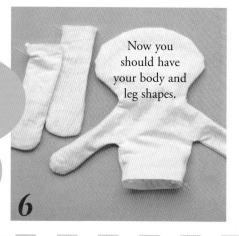

Now you should have your body and leg shapes.

6

Push in the stuffing, a little at a time.

Use a blunt pencil to ease the stuffing into areas that are difficult to reach.

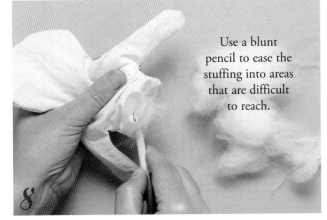

8

Stuff all the body parts.

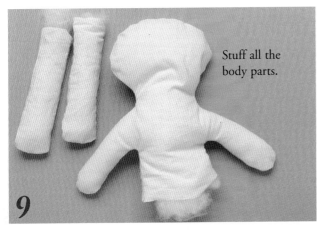

9

Turn in the edges at the base of the body and stitch it up.

10

Do the same with the legs, then sew the legs to the body.

Stuffing

Dolly is stuffed with special soft-toy stuffing. It is fluffy and lightweight and you can buy it in most craft stores.

Now you can decorate your doll.

Keep the stuffing even.

Use a backstitch to sew the legs on (page 16).

Handy tip

For a speedy finish, don't sew up the ends of the legs—simply push them up inside the body and stitch in place when you sew up the body.

Sew Dolly's faces

Now you need to make Dolly's awake and sleeping faces. Sew on the features using embroidery stitches, or try fabric pens or felt fabric for easier decoration.

You will need:

• embroidery thread
• needle
• felt pieces
• scissors
• fabric glue
• fabric pens

Sewing faces

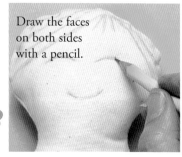

Draw the faces on both sides with a pencil.

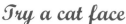

Use a backstitch for the features.

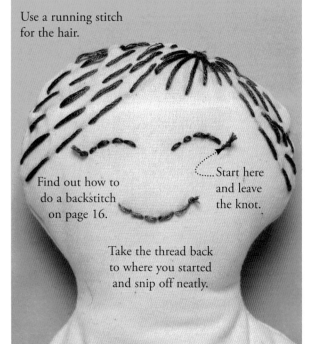

Use a running stitch for the hair.

Find out how to do a backstitch on page 16.

Start here and leave the knot.

Take the thread back to where you started and snip off neatly.

Fabric-pen faces

Fabric pens are the easiest way to put on Dolly's face.

Don't forget the eyelashes!

Felt faces

You can use felt for faces, too! Glue on using fabric glue.

Cut features out of felt.

Try a cat face

Instead of a doll, try making a teddy bear, a dog, or a cat.

Use stitches, pen, or felt pieces to decorate your cat.

Make Dolly's clothes

Now it's time to design Dolly's clothes. Pick the fabric you like and fashion together some day and night clothes.

You will need:

- pieces of fabric
- sewing thread and needle
- ribbon
- safety pins

Dolly's blouse

Dolly's skirt

Blouse

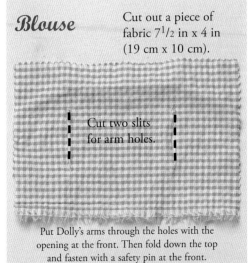

Cut out a piece of fabric 7$\frac{1}{2}$ in x 4 in (19 cm x 10 cm).

Cut two slits for arm holes.

Put Dolly's arms through the holes with the opening at the front. Then fold down the top and fasten with a safety pin at the front.

Skirt and nightie

Cut a piece of fabric 14 in x 6 in (38 cm x 15 cm).

Fold over the top and the bottom and pin in place.

Sew down the folds using running stitch (see page 16).

Sew the stitch close to the bottom of the fold.

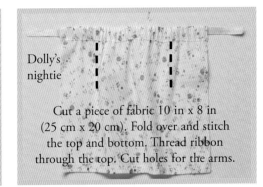

Dolly's nightie

Cut a piece of fabric 10 in x 8 in (25 cm x 20 cm). Fold over and stitch the top and bottom. Thread ribbon through the top. Cut holes for the arms.

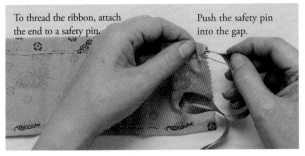

To thread the ribbon, attach the end to a safety pin.

Push the safety pin into the gap.

Push the safety pin completely through and out the other side.

Attach another safety pin to the other end of the ribbon so it doesn't pull through.

Push the fabric along the ribbon to gather it up.

Remove the safety pins.

Wrap the skirt around Dolly and tie the ribbons in a bow at the back.

Knitting

Learn to knit and you will be able to make anything from hats and scarves to bracelets and purses.

Knitting doll

Knitting dolls are a great way to knit long cords of wool.

Size 15 (10 mm) needles.

Different colored needles help you figure out which way to start knitting again when you stop half way through a row.

Size 6 (4 mm) needles.

Knitting yarn

This comes in various thicknesses and can be made from wool, nylon, or cotton. The projects in this book are mainly made from wool called double knit (DK)—not too thick and not too thin.

Needles

There are several sizes of knitting needle. The mm size refers to the thickness of the needle. When you are learning to knit, it helps to use short needles, since they are the easiest to handle.

Embroidery needles
Large needles, with blunt ends and big eyes, are best for sewing together yarn at the end of a project.

Scissors

Knitted cords

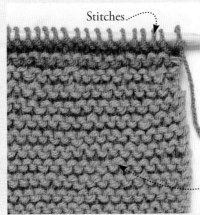

Stitches

Rows

Garter stitch

Garter stitch, or "knit stitch" is the most simple kind to learn.

Knitting

What is knitting? Knitting uses needles to work yarn into interlocking loops (stitches) to form a fabric. There are lots of stitches you can use to make fabric look different.

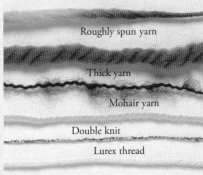

Roughly spun yarn

Thick yarn

Mohair yarn

Double knit

Lurex thread

Cotton yarn

Stocking stitch

You get this effect by knitting rows in purl stitch, then knit stitch. In this book you will learn how to do a knit stitch.

Handy knits

Can't find any knitting needles?

Then use your fingers instead. It's the handiest way to make brightly colored belts and friendship bracelets.

You will need:
- yarns—thick or thin
- your fingers

Cast on

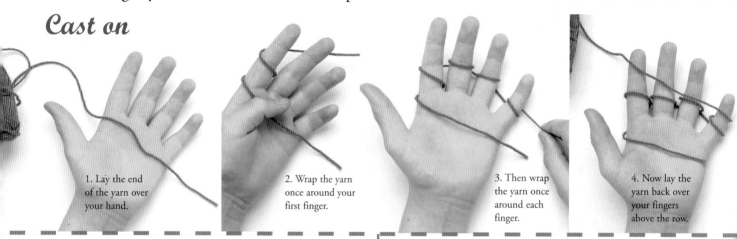

1. Lay the end of the yarn over your hand.

2. Wrap the yarn once around your first finger.

3. Then wrap the yarn once around each finger.

4. Now lay the yarn back over your fingers above the row.

Knit a row...

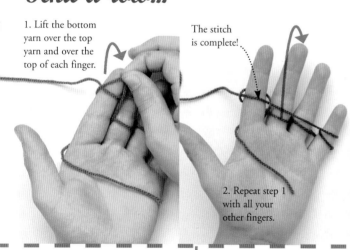

1. Lift the bottom yarn over the top yarn and over the top of each finger.

The stitch is complete!

2. Repeat step 1 with all your other fingers.

... and the next rows

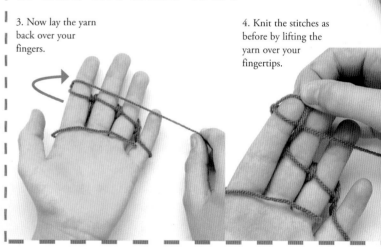

3. Now lay the yarn back over your fingers.

4. Knit the stitches as before by lifting the yarn over your fingertips.

Pull into shape

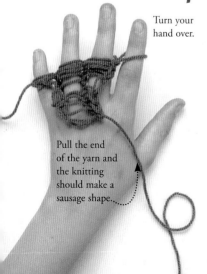

Turn your hand over.

Pull the end of the yarn and the knitting should make a sausage shape.

Finish off

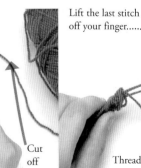

1. Lift the first stitch off your finger.

2. Put it on the next finger.

3. Knit the stitch as above by lifting one over the other.

4. Repeat this until you have one stitch left.

Cut off yarn here.

Lift the last stitch off your finger.......

Thread the end of the yarn through the loop and pull tight.

Handy tip
Don't pull the yarn too tight or it will be difficult to move the stitches on your fingers.

Mix them up
When you've got the hang of hand knitting, try mixing your colors by knitting with two or three yarns at once.

You can buy a knitting doll or make your own.

Which yarn?
Any yarn will work, but try using up leftover yarn—it's great for making long, striped cord.

The stitches are made at the top of the doll.

Knitting dolls

These are a super-simple way to make colorful cord. Turn the cord into bracelets or use it on projects in this book.

Knitting pin or embroidery needle with a blunt end

The knitted cord comes out of the bottom of the doll.

The cord is a knitted tube.

Dollies
Knitting dolls are available from toy stores and craft stores.

Make your own doll

Slip the paper clips, evenly spaced, onto the empty spool. Wrap lots of tape around them to hold them firmly in place.

You will need:

empty tape spool   4 paper clips   embroidery needle   sticky tape

Cast on

1. Take a ball of yarn and thread the end through the top of the spool.

2. Wrap the yarn around the first clip.

3. Wrap the yarn around all the clips.

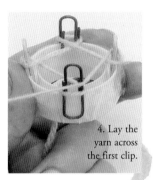

4. Lay the yarn across the first clip.

Making stitches...

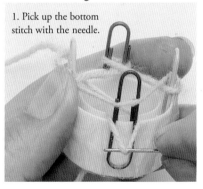

1. Pick up the bottom stitch with the needle.

2. Lift the stitch over the clip.

Continue to lay the yarn over each clip and lift each stitch over it.

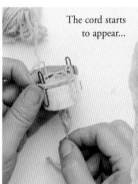

The cord starts to appear...

... Casting off

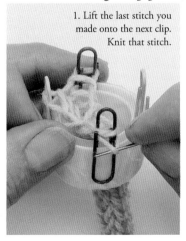

1. Lift the last stitch you made onto the next clip. Knit that stitch.

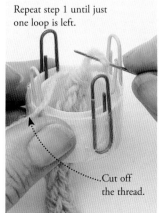

Repeat step 1 until just one loop is left.

Cut off the thread.

To finish, pass the thread through the last loop and pull it tight.

Handy tip

This homemade doll makes a thicker cord than the store-bought one.

Lots of loops

Make colorful braids
by simply tying slipknots one after the other. Use as bracelets, or accessories for your clothes.

You will need:
• yarn—scraps will do
• your fingers

Loop lots of colorful yarns at the same time.

Make a loop...

Long end

1. Wrap the end of the yarn around two fingers.

2. Make a loop in the long end of the yarn. Poke it up between your fingers.

3. Pull the loop through.

4. Pull the yarn tight to secure the loop.

... make another loop...

5. Open up the loop.

6. Pinch another loop in the long end of the yarn. Pull it through the first loop.

7. Pull the yarn tight so the second loop sits on top of the first.

... keep making loops...

Repeat steps 5, 6, and 7.

Continue until the braid is long enough to fit round your wrist.

How to stop

1. Snip off the yarn.

2. Push the end of the yarn through the last loop and pull tight.

Mix and match
Try bunching lots of yarn together and braiding as one piece. Use chunky yarn for thicker braids and shiny lurex for sparkle!

Scraps of yarn

Double yarn braid

Tie ends into a bow.

Tiny single yarn braid

Your braids make ideal friendship bracelets. Or tie them to bags or use as hair ties.

Lurex thread

Knitting with needles

Needle

Loops called stitches

Rows

Ball of yarn

Here is a piece of knitting—it has been made using a simple knitting stitch called "knit stitch." When lots of rows of knit stitch are knitted together they are known as "garter stitch."

Keep knitting and this piece will grow longer and longer.

Slip-knot

The first stitch on the needle is knotted so the yarn stays on.

Pull the ends of the yarn tight—now you have the first stitch.

Take a ball of yarn and make a loop at the end.

Bring the yarn through the loop to create a new loop.

Keep pulling the new loop through.

Attach the new loop to the needle.

Casting on
There are many ways to cast on. This method uses the thumb.

Continue doing this...

... until you have enough stitches.

Wrap the yarn around your thumb as shown.

Pick up the yarn with the needle.

Let the yarn go from your thumb onto the needle.

How many?
The projects in this book tell you how many stitches to cast on. Lots of stitches give you a wide fabric, while few stitches make a narrow fabric.

Now you are ready to KNIT!

Stitches 1 2 3 4 5...

When you are starting a new row, start with the first stitch on the right and work toward the left.

The yarn will be on the right as well.

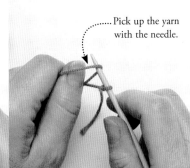

How to knit "knit stitch"

Two ways to knit—the steps below show two different ways to do a knit stitch. Try them and see which method suits you best. Left-handers often find the second method easiest.

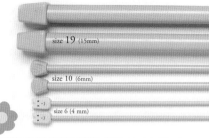

size 19 (15mm)

size 10 (6mm)

size 6 (4 mm)

1 Try this way... There's a rhyme by the numbers below. Learn it—it might help you remember how to knit!

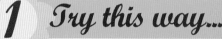

Stitches cast on ready for knitting

Try putting the yarn between the fingers on your right hand so you don't have to move your whole hand to make a stitch.

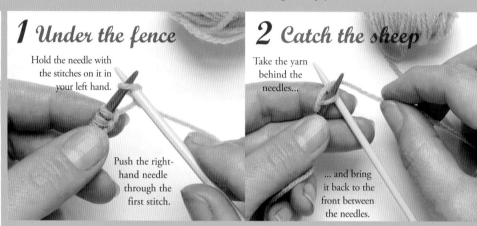

1 Under the fence

Hold the needle with the stitches on it in your left hand.

Push the right-hand needle through the first stitch.

2 Catch the sheep

Take the yarn behind the needles...

... and bring it back to the front between the needles.

2 ... or this way Try this if you are left-handed.

Stitches cast on ready for knitting

Place the yarn around the fingers of your left hand as shown.

1 Into the bunnyhole

Hold the needle with stitches on it in your left hand.

Push the right-hand needle through the first stitch.

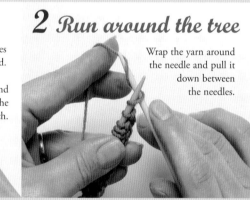

2 Run around the tree

Wrap the yarn around the needle and pull it down between the needles.

Casting off—how to stop Take away the stitches one by one.

1. Knit two stitches.

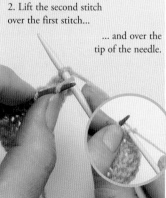

2. Lift the second stitch over the first stitch...

... and over the tip of the needle.

REPEAT steps 1 and 2 until only one stitch remains on the needle.

TO FINISH OFF, open up the stitch, snip off the ball of yarn, and put the end of the yarn back through the loop.

Pull the thread tight.

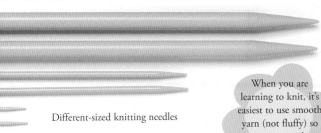

Different-sized knitting needles

When you are learning to knit, it's easiest to use smooth yarn (not fluffy) so you can see what you're doing.

You will need:

ball of yarn — scissors — needle threader — embroidery needle

3 Back we go

Twist the tip of the right-hand needle toward the front bringing the yarn with it.

4 Off we leap

Pull the new stitch off the left-hand needle.

When the row is complete...

Repeat steps 1, 2, 3, 4.

... swap the needles so that the knitting is in your left hand.

3 Out of the bunnyhole

Bring the right-hand needle to the front bringing the yarn with it.

4 Away runs he

Pull the new stitch off the left-hand needle.

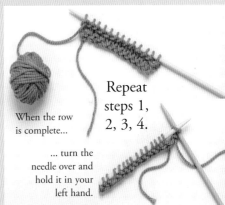

When the row is complete...

Repeat steps 1, 2, 3, 4.

... turn the needle over and hold it in your left hand.

Sew in yarn ends

Thread each end onto an embroidery needle.

Push the needle down through the edge of the knitting—about the first five rows.

When the piece of knitting is complete, neaten it up by sewing in the ends.

Snip off the yarn.

Sew up seams

Place two pieces of knitting together.

Knot the yarn and sew it so it goes inside the seam.

Sew over the edge of the knitting—then fasten off by sewing down the edge.

Cut off thread.

Krazy knits

Knit simple strips and use them to create your own zany friends.

You will need:

- Size 6 (4 mm) knitting needles
- yarn • felt scraps • fabric glue
- knitted cords • embroidery needle
- soft-toy stuffing

Sew in strand as shown on page 53.

Fill up with stuffing.

Cast on 12 stitches.
Knit to length of 5 in (13 cm).

Fold the strip in half and sew up the sides leaving the top open.

1 Knit a strip

2 Fold it in half

3 Stuff it

Sew up the opening.

Fabric glue

Cut some face shapes out of felt and glue them in place with fabric glue.

Decide where to put the pieces before you stick them down.

4 Sew it up

5 Give it a face

Legs and tails
Use cords from the knitting doll project (page 48) and stitch them on as legs and tails.

Cute cat

All-arms alien

Krazy Kat

Krazy Kat
To make Krazy Kat, knit a longer strip 9 in (23 cm) and follow the steps as before. Give him a head by tying a piece of yarn around him then pulling it in tight.

Owls

Knitted purses

From knitted strips to handy bags.

Simple but useful, these little bags can be made to any size that suits you.

You will need:
- Size 6 (4 mm) knitting needles
- yarn • embroidery needle
- buttons

1 Knit a strip

Sew the end in as shown on page 53.

Knit this strip
Cast on 15 stitches and keep knitting until your strip is 6 in (15 cm) long.

Sew the end in as shown on page 53.

2 Stitch it up

Bag size
To make a larger or smaller bag, simply cast on more or fewer stitches and knit a longer or shorter strip.

This will form the flap of the bag.

Sew up the sides with yarn.

Fold the bottom of the bag up, as shown, leaving a flap.

3 Make a loop

1. Pass a threaded needle through the center of the flap.

Don't pull it all the way through.

2. Pull one strand of yarn through so the yarn is on either side of the bag.

3. Knot the two strands together to make the loop.

Bring your purse alive by giving it a face. Glue on felt shapes or sew buttons for eyes.

Make a long cord to hang the bag around your neck.

Sew on a button to keep the bag shut.........

Handy tip
Use your knitting doll cords (page 48) to make a strap. Put the end of the cord just inside the top of the bag and sew into place.

Woolen hats

A hat for you and a hat for Dolly!

Stitch the end back into the strip (see page 53).

1 Knit a strip

Cast on 16 stitches and knit to 8 in (20 cm) in length.

Use size 6 (4 mm) needles for Dolly's hat.

You will need:
- knit a strip (see how to knit on page 52)
- embroidery needle
- felt flowers and pom-poms (for decoration)
- sewing needle and thread

Knot the end of the yarn.

Sew a running stitch around the top edge of the hat.

2 Fold it in half

Sew the two edges together.

3 Gather one end of the hat

Pull the yarn tightly to gather up the opening.

Sew backward and forward over the gathers to keep them together.

Felt flowers on page 32...

See how to make pom-poms on page 61.

Cut out felt shapes.

Sew the decorations to the hat with a sewing needle and thread.

4 Secure the hat top

5 Ready to decorate

Use Size 10 (6 mm) needles for your hat.

A hat for you

Follow the steps for Dolly's hat—just make yours bigger! Using size 10 (6 mm) needles, cast on 30 stitches and knit to 20 in (50 cm) in length. Finish off the hat in the same way as Dolly's, then decorate.

Knit another strip to make Dolly a cozy scarf.

Pom-poms

Find out how to make pom-poms on page 61. To attach them to your hats, simply sew with a needle and thread. To make small pom-poms, cut out small cardboard disks about 2 in (5 cm).

Big knitting!

Big needles—big difference!
Try them and see.

Size 6
(4 mm
needle)

Size 19
(15 mm
needle)

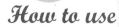

How to use
Use large needles
in the same
way as small ones.
And remember—
the thinner the
yarn, the looser
the knit will be.

You will need:
• big needles size 19 (15 mm)
• 200 gm ball of double-
  knit yarn

Pom-poms

You will need:
• two disks of cardboard
• knitting yarn

Cut out two cardboard disks 5 in (12 cm).

Put the two disks together and wrap the yarn around and around the cardboard.

Pinch the middle. Slip the scissors between the disks and cut the yarn.

Slide a piece of yarn between the disks. Wrap it around the cut yarn.

Pull the yarn tight and knot the ends together.

Pull off the pieces of cardboard.

Big scarf

Make your knitting long enough for a scarf and finish it off with pom-poms.

To attach a pom-pom, gather up the end of the scarf and sew on the pom-pom using an embroidery needle and same-colored yarn.

Leg pattern

SOLID LINE shows
where to cut out the
pattern and your fabric...

DOTTED LINE shows
where to sew your project.

Dolly pattern

Here is the pattern for the doll on page 38.

It's shown here actual size, so simply trace the patterns and cut
out the material to match.

These "V" shapes show
where to snip the fabric
to help shape the doll.

You will need:
• tracing paper • pen • scissors
• pins • fabric